Blunder or I

Fact & Fiction of Famous Inventors and Inventions

by Nancy Polette

Illustrated by Paul Dillon

© 2006 Nancy Polette
CLC0402
ISBN 1-931334-91-9
Published by Pieces of Learning

All rights reserved. In our effort to produce high quality educational products we offer portions of this book as "reproducible." Permission is granted, therefore, to the buyer - one teacher - to reproduce student activity pages in LIMITED quantities for students in the buyer's classroom only. The right to reproduce is not extended to other teachers, entire schools, or to school systems. Use of any pages on the Internet is strictly forbidden. No other part of this publication may be reproduced in whole or part. The whole publication may not be stored in a retrieval system, or transmitted in any form or by any means, electronic, mechanical, photocopying, recording, or otherwise without written permission of the author or publisher.
For any other use contact Pieces of Learning at 1-800-729-5137. For a complete catalog of products contact Pieces of Learning or visit our Web Site at
www.piecesoflearning.com

Table of Contents

Archimedes made one of his greatest discoveries in his bath. 5
The first automobile had a top speed of 20 miles per hour. 7
The Band-Aid® was invented for a clumsy wife. 9
Alexander Graham Bell taught his dog to talk. 11
Blue Jeans were invented to get rid of canvas no one wanted. 13
Louis Braille developed his Braille system for the blind at age 15. 15
Luther Burbank, the plant doctor, could do only one experiment at a time. 17
George Washington Carver had a secret garden 19
A defeated general led to the invention of chewing gum. 21
The invention of Chocolate Chip Cookies was an accident. 23
Coca-Cola® was once sold as a brain tonic. 25
People lined up to buy Samuel Colt's first revolver. 27
The first computer program was written by a woman in 1843. 29
Cough drops once paid for a meal 31
Thomas Alva Edison invented gummed paper. 33
Elisha Otis was a daredevil. 35
The flashlight grew out of a flowerpot. 37
Benjamin Franklin had only two years of schooling. 39
Robert Fulton was a doodler. 41
Robert Goddard's rockets helped win World War II. 43
The Hershey® Bar was developed in a university laboratory. 45
The Hula Hoop saved the jobs of hundreds of workers. 47
Horace Wells discovered laughing gas as a pain killer. 49
Marconi, inventor of the telegraph, failed his university entrance exams. 51
The first friction match was three feet long. 53
The "Real McCoy" was an invention by a cowboy hero. 55
The microwave oven was an accident. 57
Anton Leeuwenhoek shared his invention of the microscope with others. 59
Samuel Morse was awarded a gold medal for his art. 61
Alfred Nobel, the inventor of dynamite, gave money for a peace prize. 63
André Garnerin used a parachute to escape from prison. 65
An angry cook invented potato chips. 67
The invention of the printing press made Gutenberg a wealthy man. 69
The refrigerator was invented for yellow fever patients. 71
The first traffic light had three lights: stop, go, and caution. 73
Velcro® came about from a walk in the woods. 75
Neither of the Wright Brothers received a high school diploma. 77
Bibliography 79

FACT OR FICTION?

Archimedes made one of his greatest discoveries in his bath.

The task of a man of renown

Was to seek out the gold in a crown

Submerged in his bath

The man did the math

And went running all bare through the town.

Archimedes made one of his greatest discoveries in his bath.

Archimedes (287-212 B.C.)
"The Wise One"

Archimedes invented many useful things. He figured out how to lift objects with a lever and pulley. He invented a screw to raise water to irrigate fields. He invented the catapult to hold back approaching armies. Sometimes when he wasn't inventing he played with math problems. He drew math problems in the dirt. He drew math problems in the ashes from a fire. He drew math problems in the oil from his bath.

It was in his bath that Archimedes made one of his greatest discoveries. Archimedes and the King of Syracuse were best friends. The king decided he wanted a new crown. Not any crown would do. The new crown had to be made entirely of gold. The King gave a local goldsmith the gold that he was to use, and he set about the task of creating the crown.

When the crown was delivered, the King suspected that the goldsmith kept some of the gold for himself and used silver in part of the crown. It looked like a gold crown. It felt like a gold crown. But was it really all gold? The King had to know. He called on his good friend Archimedes. If anyone could discover silver in the crown, Archimedes could.

Archimedes thought about the problem for a long time. He did not want to disappoint the King, but he could think of no way to determine if the crown contained silver. Pondering the problem, he stepped into his bath. As he sank down into the bath, the water rose in the same proportion as the amount of his body that was under water.

"Eureka!" he shouted. The suspicious crown should displace the same amount of water as a gold crown of the same size. If the crown contained silver, it would displace a different amount of water. An excited Archimedes jumped out of the bath and ran through the streets of Syracuse shouting *"Eureka, Eureka."* There was one slight problem. He forgot to put on his clothes!

FACT OR FICTION?

The first automobile had a top speed of 20 miles per hour.

There once was a fellow who tried

To invent a machine that would ride

With power, of course

Instead of a horse

And a pretty girl right by his side.

The first automobile had a top speed of 20 miles per hour.

The First Automobile did not break any speed records!

For years people laughed at the idea of a horseless carriage. They made up silly songs and poems about it. *"Nothing,"* people said, *"Could ever replace the horse."*

Many inventors tried to build a horseless carriage. The earliest ancestor on record of a modern automobile was built in France in 1771. It had two problems. It took a mechanical genius to operate it, and its top speed was three miles an hour. Horses could go faster than that! Needless to say, it did not catch the public's fancy. Perhaps that is why its inventor, Nicholas Cugnot, is long forgotten.

One hundred years later in 1873 another inventor, Amédée Bollée, tried to take credit for the first automobile. He built a 12-passenger car powered by a steam engine. It needed someone to keep a wood fire going all the time to produce steam. The car needed a driver and a stoker and could not go very fast. People preferred the horse and buggy.

The first practical automobile with a gasoline engine was built in 1889 by two sharp fellows (the same year, but in two different places) named Gottlieg Daimler and Karl Benz. Their automobiles could go an amazing 10 miles per hour. Of course, there were no paved roads or handy gas stations, so only a few were purchased.

Seven years later in 1896, Henry Ford built a gasoline-powered car. He saw into the future with paved roads and gasoline stations everywhere. He wanted to make the automobile available to everyone, not just the rich. He invented the assembly line, a way to turn out automobiles as cheaply as possible. Henry Ford lived to see his dream come true. In the next 18 years he produced and sold eighteen million Model T Fords!

FACT OR FICTION?

The Band-Aid® was invented for a clumsy wife.

A fellow named Earle took a wife

For she was the love of his life

Then he learned with a groan

She was accident prone

Whenever she picked up a knife.

The Band-Aid® was invented for a clumsy wife.

Band-Aids®
A million dollar invention!

In 1920, young Earle Dickson had a very good job. He worked as a cotton buyer for a company named Johnson and Johnson. The company made gauze and adhesive tape for bandages. Gauze is made from cotton. Only 40 years before people used corn husks for bandages.

Earle had such a good job that he decided it was time to get married. He had his eye on a pretty girl named Josephine for quite a while. It was a good thing that Josephine had her eye on Earle. When he asked her to marry him she said *"YES!"*

Earle soon found out that Josephine and knives didn't get along. It didn't matter if it was a steak knife, a paring knife, or a butcher knife. Whenever Josephine picked up a knife, she managed to cut herself. The first week Earle and Josephine were married she cut herself twice. Earle got out the gauze, cut some from the roll, wrapped it around Josephine's finger, and secured it with adhesive tape.

While Earle and Josephine got along just fine, Josephine and knives never did get along. Josephine was an accident waiting to happen, and the accidents happened more often than not. Earle got very good at bandaging up Josephine's wounds.

Then one day when Josephine cut herself again, Earle got an idea. He snipped off and folded up a small piece of gauze. He tore off a strip of adhesive tape. He placed the gauze in the center of the tape and wrapped the tape around Josephine's finger. It was fast, it was easy, it saved on gauze and tape, and best of all, it worked! Johnson & Johnson liked Earle's idea so much that they started making Band-Aids®. Earle got a promotion. He became vice president of the company (thanks to a clumsy wife!)

FACT OR FICTION?

Alexander Graham Bell taught his dog to talk.

There once was a fellow named Bell

Who worked with vibrations so well

Many years were well spent

So that he could invent

A machine through which people could yell.

Alexander Graham Bell taught his dog to talk.

Alexander Graham Bell (1847-1922)
He sent speech over wire.

"Smart Alex! Smart Alex!" the boys yelled at Alexander. The boy ignored the teasing. His mother did not hear the taunts. She was deaf.

Alexander couldn't help being smart. When he did not have his nose in a book, he liked to hear his mother play the piano. Alex wondered, *"How could she play music she could not hear? Did she feel the vibrations from the piano?"* If so, perhaps she could feel the vibrations from his voice if Alex spoke close to her forehead. He tried it, and she did.

Alex continued to experiment with vibrations. When his dog growled, Alex held the dog's throat and tongue in such a way that the growls sounded like words. Of course, the dog was not really talking, but that is what it sounded like.

In the 1840s, a deaf person learned sign language to communicate. Alex decided to spend his life helping the deaf speak. He became a teacher of the deaf. Always open to new ideas, he was fascinated with the invention of the telegraph that sent signals over a wire. If dots and dashes could travel over wire, why not words?

On March 6, 1876, Bell was hard at work in his laboratory. He connected wires and turned knobs on a speech transmitter. His assistant, Thomas Watson, worked in another room. Imagine a startled Watson when he heard the words, "Come here, Watson, I want you."

The words came through a receiver nearby. They were the first words to ever travel along a wire. It was amazing. It was astounding! The teacher of the deaf invented a way for the hearing to talk to each other over distance. It was the first telephone.

FACT OR FICTION?

Blue Jeans were invented to get rid of canvas no one wanted.

Strauss was a fellow quite smart

Who traveled around in a cart

Then one day he went

And cut up a tent

Making pants that would

not come apart.

Blue Jeans were invented to get rid of canvas no one wanted.

Levi Strauss (1829-1902)
He found a new use for canvas.

In 1849, people from all over the country rushed to California to stake a gold claim. Levi Strauss traveled all the way across the ocean to the United States from the country of Bavaria. He staked a claim of a different kind.

Levi knew that one thing everyone needed was clothing. Young or old, rich or poor, folks needed to be covered up. In Levi's day clothing was sewn by hand. Women bought yards of cloth, measured, and cut, and sewed clothes for their families. Rich women bought yards of cloth and paid dressmakers to make their gowns.

Levi headed west with bolts of cloth. He also took sheets of canvas. He figured miners would need canvas for tents and wagon covers. Strauss sold his bolts of cloth to the few women in the camps, but he could not sell the canvas. Miners were too busy searching for gold to care about tents and wagon covers.

One day Levi stood looking at the canvas he could not sell. ZOUNDS! A great idea popped into his head. Miners did rough, dirty work. Pants wore out in a hurry. What if miners had pants that didn't wear out for a very long time? What if they had canvas pants? Levi measured, and cut, and sewed canvas pants. The miners liked the pants. More and more men asked Levi to make pants for them.

In 1898, Levi Strauss opened a factory in San Francisco. From France he got a heavy material called "genes." He put copper rivets in spots where the pants might show wear. He called his pants "Levi's®." The people who bought and wore them soon gave them a new name, "Blue Jeans." Levi Strauss would be astonished to know that they are one of the best selling items in the world today.

FACT OR FICTION?

Louis Braille developed his Braille system for the blind at age 15.

Braille was a bright lad indeed

Who learned all his lessons with speed

He worked lots and lots

With funny raised dots

So those without sight could now read.

Louis Braille developed his Braille system for the blind at age 15.

Louis Braille (1809-1852)
He taught the blind to read.

Lively Louis walked and talked long before most babies. By age three he could carry on a conversation with almost anyone. It was also at age three that Louis became blind. Playing in his father's workshop, the small boy rounded a corner too fast and connected with a sharp object. It pierced his eye. His frantic parents sought the best medical help they could find. In 1812, with no antibiotics and little medical knowledge, the eye became infected. The infection spread to the other eye, and young Louis lost his sight.

There were no schools for blind children in the small French town where Louis lived. This did not stop his parents from wanting their child to have the best education possible. They sent Louis to the local school. He learned by listening and became the top pupil in his class.

At the age of 10 Louis enrolled in a school for the blind in Paris. The boy soaked up learning like a sponge. In addition to his studies he learned to play the piano and the organ. Imagine learning to play those instruments without being able to see the notes!

In 1821, an army captain visited the school. He brought with him a method of raised dots for reading and writing. The raised dots fascinated Louis. For three years he studied them intensely. He worked out the many problems with the system and used it to develop his own practical system of touch reading using only six raised dots. He named it the Braille System. He was 15 years old.

Unfortunately, it was only after his death that the Braille System became the most valuable way to teach the blind to read. Today the Braille System is used all over the world. By touching the raised dots, many blind people can read faster than those with sight...thanks to Louis Braille.

FACT OR FICTION?

Luther Burbank, the plant doctor,
could do only one experiment
at a time.

A plant genius, he filled a gap

For creating new fruits was a snap

He'd combine different seeds

And create brand new breeds

And put a new plant on the map.

Luther Burbank, the plant doctor, could do only one experiment at a time.

Luther Burbank (1849-1926)
The father of the Idaho Potato

Luther Burbank never attended high school. He never attended college. Yet he became the most famous plant scientist of his day. Luther grew up on a family farm in Massachusetts. Before, during, and after his farm chores the boy could be found with his nose in a book. He read, and he read, and he learned. While most teenage boys dreamed about girls, Luther dreamed about plants.

Twenty-one-year-old Luther bought 17 acres of land where he could experiment with plants. He grafted seedlings into fully developed plants and created new plants. At one time he had 3,000 experiments going at the same time. He developed more than 800 new plants including hundreds of varieties of fruits and flowers. He liked the challenge of a difficult problem and worked until he solved each one. Many people brought Luther their plant problems.

In many areas of the West it is difficult to grow feed for cattle. One thing that does grow well in the West is cactus. Cactus would be good feed except for the thorns. Burbank solved the problem by creating a cactus without thorns.

In Ireland the potatoes were the only food many had. To remain in their small cottages, the Irish paid their rent with potatoes. But the potatoes turned black in the ground. Burbank created a potato that was strong enough to resist the blight that caused potatoes to rot. This new potato saved the lives and homes of thousands of Irish. Today we call it the Idaho potato. Whether you like it mashed, baked, or fried, the next time you dig into one, thank Luther Burbank.

FACT OR FICTION?

George Washington Carver had a secret garden.

George Washington Carver the man

Over a fifty year span

Useful products he found

From plants in the ground

When he said, "I think that I can."

George Washington Carver had a secret garden.

George Washington Carver (1864-1943)
The slave who changed farmers' lives

In 1864, raiders rode on to Moses Carver's farm. They made off with a slave woman and her baby. The next day a Union scout found the baby but not the mother. Moses Carver gave the scout a horse as a thank you for finding the baby. The baby's name was George Washington Carver.

For a while it didn't look like little George would live. He needed a lot of nursing. Since Mrs. Carver spent many hours looking after George, she discovered this little boy was very bright. Something had to be done. George should go to school. Sad to say, the local school refused to take George. Why? He was black. The Carvers tried to teach him at home, but he soon learned all they could teach him. When he was 10, the Carvers sent him to a school for black children in a nearby town. Before leaving, George showed them the garden he had grown in secret for more than five years. Strange plants grew in well-kept rows. The Carvers promised to take care of the garden until George returned.

George worked hard in grade school and high school. He dreamed of going to college. Once again, no college would have him because of his color. George did not give up. Finally, Simpson College in Iowa let 30-year-old George enroll as a freshman. Within a short time George knew more than the professors.

George had another dream. He wanted to find many uses for common crops so the poor farmers of the South would have better markets for the things they grew. As a professor at Tuskegee University he spent countless hours in his plant laboratory. He found over 280 products that could be made from the peanut including flour, rubber, and instant coffee. He discovered many uses for sweet potatoes and soybeans. When new markets opened, Southern farmers began to raise peanuts, sweet potatoes, and soybeans instead of cotton.

The little boy, born a slave, saved the family farms of many farmers. Before his death he gave one more contribution. All of his life's savings were given to Tuskegee Institute. His work continues there to this day.

FACT OR FICTION?

A defeated general led to the invention of chewing gum.

Tom Adams was under great stress
As he worked with a rubbery mess
Till a package of chicle
He sold for a nickle
His gum was an instant success!

A defeated general led to the invention of chewing gum.

Thomas Adams (1818-1905)
The Chewing Gum Man

Nearly everyone has heard of the Battle of the Alamo where a small group of brave defenders held out for 11 days against 4,000 troops of General Santa Anna. While the General claimed victory at the Alamo, he was defeated in a later battle and left Mexico for Staten Island, New York. There he stayed in the home of Thomas Adams.

As an inventor, Thomas tinkered with lots of ideas but did not have the money to carry them out. Santa Anna suggested that cheap and plentiful chicle from Mexico might make good rubber. A cheaper, stronger, more durable rubber would make Adams a fortune.

Thomas thought this was a great idea. Santa Anna still had friends in Mexico. He arranged for a large quantity of chicle to be shipped to Thomas Adams.

Thomas rented a warehouse to store the chicle. He worked day and night to come up with a cheaper kind of rubber. He tried making toys, and boots, and bicycle tires. Nothing worked. The rubber split and came apart. It would not keep its shape. After months of work Adams decided the best place for all that chicle was at the bottom of the East River.

Many inventions come from accidental discoveries. Wondering what to do with all the chicle in the warehouse, Thomas broke off a piece and popped it in his mouth. He enjoyed chewing the chicle. Maybe other people would enjoy it, too. Adams told his sons about his idea. They made up boxes of the chicle gum. A local druggist agreed to sell the gum. It was a hit!

Two years later Thomas invented a machine to make the gum and opened the first chewing gum factory in the country. Before long factory workers were adding different flavors to the gum, and it became popular throughout the nation. Adams had finally found success as an inventor, thanks to a defeated general.

FACT OR FICTION?

The invention of Chocolate Chip Cookies was an accident.

A lady named Ruth tried to bake

Some cookies instead of a cake

She broke up some strips

And made chocolate chips

A surprisingly yummy mistake.

The invention of Chocolate Chip Cookies was an accident.

Ruth Wakefield (1903-1977)
Inventor of Chocolate Chip Cookies

Did you know that people have been eating chocolate chip cookies for more than 70 years? More than seven billion are eaten every year. It is the most popular cookie in America. Yet, the chocolate chip cookie came about by accident.

A long time ago in 1930, Ruth Wakefield and her husband owned a small inn in Massachusetts. They named it the Toll House Inn. Ruth cooked all of the meals and desserts. People went out of their way to stop by the Inn and sample Ruth's chocolate cookies.

One morning Ruth needed to bake a batch of chocolate cookies. In went the flour, and the brown sugar, and the eggs, and the butter. Ruth reached for the baking chocolate. There wasn't any! Ruth could not leave her baking to go to the store. Then she had an idea. A friend, Andrew Nestle, had given her a candy bar of semi-sweet chocolate. If she broke it up and put small pieces in the cookie batter the pieces would melt and she would have chocolate cookies.

Imagine Ruth's surprise when the chocolate bits did not melt! Ruth saw chips of chocolate scattered in the cookies. Would the people who bought her famous chocolate cookies like these? They did and asked for more!

Ruth named her new cookie the Toll House® Cookie after the Inn. You can find Ruth's cookie recipe today on every bag of Nestle's® chocolate chips.

FACT OR FICTION?

Coca-Cola® was once sold as a brain tonic.

John Pemberton's popular drink

He mixed up as quick as a wink

If he gave some to you

Just a quick sip or two

Will make you forget how to think.

Coca-Cola® was once sold as a brain tonic.

John Pemberton (1830-1888)
His brain tonic, Coca-Cola®, put people to sleep!

Medicine Man shows are featured in many Western movies. The Medicine Man pulls his wagon into town, puts on a show, and then tries to convince folks to buy his bottled medicine, guaranteed to cure any ailment. The medicine usually did make folks forget their aches and pains for a short while since it contained alcohol. When the effect of the alcohol wore off, the aches and pains came back. By this time the Medicine Man had left town.

John Pemberton mixed up his medicines in Atlanta, Georgia. While he did not put on a traveling Medicine Man show, he liked stirring up different syrups and mixtures. His most popular mixture was called "French Wine of Coca." It contained wine, the drug cocaine, and caffeine. He advertised it as a brain tonic. A lot of people liked the way the drink made them feel. They didn't worry about their brains.

In 1885, John had a problem. Alcohol was banned in Atlanta. He had to remove the wine from his poplar drink. In its place he added sugar and oils from several fruits. Not too many people liked the new drink so John sold the recipe. The same recipe was sold twice more when the third buyer, Asa Chandler, put bubbles in the drink. He named it Coca-Cola® and people loved it.

Today Coca-Cola® (without the cocaine) is one of the most popular drinks in the world. If you wonder what its ingredients are you will have to keep on wondering. The recipe for making Coca-Cola® is a heavily guarded secret.

FACT OR FICTION?

People lined up to buy Samuel Colt's first revolver.

Sam Colt was a lad much admired

Mechanical skills he acquired

He toyed with a gun

'Til a cylinder spun

And multiple shots could be fired.

People lined up to buy Samuel Colt's first revolver.

Samuel Colt (1814-1862)
He invented the revolver.

Sam Colt liked to tinker. Much to his parent's dismay he took every new toy apart to see how it worked. Wherever Sam was, mechanical parts were scattered all around him. The boy especially enjoyed taking apart his father's firearms. He spent hours discovering just how the guns were put together. Fortunately, if Sam took something apart he always put it together again.

Sam was too busy tinkering to have time for book learning. He thought school was a waste of time. At age 15 he signed on with a ship's crew and went to sea. Legend says that it was at sea that he got the idea for a gun that could shoot more than once before reloading. He watched the ship's wheel turn round and round. Why couldn't a pistol have a revolving wheel or cylinder that would drop bullets into the chamber one at a time? Four years later Sam invented the first revolver, a gun that could shoot multiple times.

In New Jersey, Sam set up a factory to manufacture the gun. It was an excellent, well-made gun. Unfortunately it was so new and different that few people wanted to buy it. Sam lost most of his money and closed the factory. Sam did not give up. He kept on tinkering. His tinkering made possible remote control explosions and underwater cable.

Fortunately for Sam the Army heard about his revolvers. The Army wanted to buy large quantities of his revolvers. Sam set up another factory. The Colt name became known all over the world for quality and dependability. The boy who liked to tinker became a very rich man.

FACT OR FICTION?

The first computer program was written by a woman in 1843.

There was a young lady it seems

Who thought that computers were dreams

Till she got out her pen

Calculated and then

Came up with mathematical schemes.

The first computer program was written by a woman in 1843.

Ada Lovelace (1815-1852)
She predicted the future.

Ada Lovelace was the daughter of Lord Byron, the famous poet. Famous or not, Ada's mother left Lord Byron to raise her daughter alone. Ada's mother had little use for poets. Her daughter would be a scientist! She filled Ada's childhood with lessons in math and science, and Ada learned the lessons well!

A grown-up Ada met a man named Mr. Babbage. He had a revolutionary idea for a calculating engine. Ada's eyes sparkled as Mr. Babbage explained his idea. Ada and Babbage wrote back and forth for two years. In one of her letters she laid out a plan for how his machine might work. The year was 1843. This was the first computer program ever written!

Ada married and had three children but continued her interest in science and mathematics. Ada loved horses, she loved music, but most of all she loved calculating machines. She predicted that someday such a machine might be used to compose and play music and draw pictures as well as calculating numbers.

A lot of folks thought Ada was a foolish dreamer. In her wildest dreams Ada could not have imagined a time when the computer would be in every home. One hundred and thirty years later, Steve Jobs and Steve Wozniak made their home computer dream a reality. The two friends were designing computer games when they got the idea for a personal computer. They worked together in a garage and came up with a model they thought they could sell. It had no memory or keyboard but worked quite well. The two named the computer Apple and sold almost everything they owned to get the money to make 50 of them. They sold all fifty. Within six years both Steves had become millionaires!

Ada probably would have said, *"I told you so!"*

FACT OR FICTION?

Cough drops once paid for a meal.

A businessman made a good swap

With a poor man who happened to stop

For a meal one fine day

But then he couldn't pay

Except with a candy cough drop.

Cough drops once paid for a meal.

Smith Brothers® Cough Drops
An overnight success

In 1847, folks in Poughkeepsie, New York, could get a good meal at a good price at James Smith's restaurant. For dessert they could try some of James' delicious candy. James was an excellent candymaker.

It was common back then for peddlers to travel from one town to another selling everything from pots and pans to ladies' corsets. Sly Hawkins traveled all day without a sale. He was tired, he was hungry, and he was broke. He smelled the wonderful aromas coming from James Smith's restaurant. He went in, sat down, and ordered a meal. He took his time and ate every bite. When it came time to pay for the meal he had no money. *"Not to worry,"* he said to James. *"I have this formula for a cough candy. Guaranteed to stop a cough, a cold, sore throat, asthma, and numerous other ailments."* He offered to trade the cough candy formula for his meal.

James thought cough candy was a good idea. He tore up the restaurant bill and gave the man five dollars. The next morning James cooked up a batch of cough candy. He put the candy in small envelopes and sent his two boys, William and Andrew, out on the streets to sell it. Sell it they did! The cough candy was such a success that William and Andrew formed the Smith Brothers® Company. To protect their formula the Smith brothers put their pictures on the package. It happened that the word "Trade" was under William's picture and the word "Mark" was under Andrew's picture. People thought the men who made the cough candy were named Trade and Mark.

The cough drops were so successful that you can still find them on drugstore shelves today thanks to a peddler who had no money.

FACT OR FICTION?

Thomas Alva Edison invented gummed paper.

His teachers thought he wasn't bright

In third grade from school he took flight

For Tom was a thinker

And he liked to tinker

Creating a long-lasting light.

Thomas Alva Edison invented gummed paper.

Thomas Alva Edison (1847-1931)
He made the world a brighter place.

Almost everyone gives Thomas Edison credit for inventing the first practical light bulb. Few people know he should also be thanked for inventing gummed paper.

One day Edison was gluing paper together in his laboratory. Glue got all over his hands. He thought about the problem. He spread some glue on paper and let it dry. Then he slightly moistened the glue to see if it would stick. It did. Thanks to Thomas Edison we have stamps that stick to envelopes and sticky notes to remind us of the things we need to do.

It is true that Thomas only went to third grade in school. His teachers thought he was dull. They did not realize that the young boy had a hearing problem. His mother taught him at home, and he taught himself by reading a whole set of encyclopedias. Edison's curiosity often got him in trouble. He set fire to his father's barn to see what would happen. He set up a laboratory in his basement but had to give it up. His mother could not stand the smell that came from it.

Edison got a job as a train boy but nearly burned down a freight car with his experiments. Never discouraged, young Thomas continued to experiment with anything electrical. For a time he had no money and borrowed money from his father. Eventually his experiments paid off, and he made enough money to set up a real working laboratory.

In 1877, he invented the phonograph and the phonograph record. He invented the movie projector and gummed paper as well as improving the electric light. The teachers who had labeled Thomas "dull" would have been amazed to know that because of his inventions the world became a brighter (and less sticky) place.

FACT OR FICTION?

Elisha Otis was a daredevil!

A man at the New York World's Fair
Performed way up high in the air
He came down with a jerk
Safety brakes were at work
But he gave the folks watching a scare.

Elisha Otis was a daredevil!

Elisha Otis (1811-1861)
He built the first safe elevator.

    Visitors at New York World's Fair wanted to see the daredevil! The year was 1854. Crowds flocked to the Crystal Palace to watch a man take his life in his hands. Elisha Otis stood on a platform. The platform, pulled by ropes, rose higher and higher until it reached a height of more than 100 feet. Elisha cut the ropes! Some women hid their eyes. Men gasped. The platform would surely crash to the ground killing the man aboard. The platform started down. Faster and faster it went. Then with a grinding screech it stopped in mid flight. Two metal hands reached out and grabbed the platform. Otis smiled. He was not a daredevil. He knew all the time he would be safe. He had invented the first safety elevator!

    Elevators had been around for a very long time. In 1743, King Louis XV had an elevator built in his palace. Men pulling ropes hoisted him from one floor to another. Woe to the man who let go of a rope! The king would get a much faster ride than he expected.

    Three years before Otis gave his "daredevil" demonstration he worked in a factory that made beds. The owner asked him to design an elevator that could take the beds from one floor to another. Elisha designed and built two metal hands to reach out and stop the elevator if the ropes broke. Unfortunately, the owner of the bed factory went broke. Fortunately, Elisha was able to buy the factory and build more elevators. Lots of companies wanted them after seeing how Elisha made them safe.

    Imagine a big city today without elevators. The skyscrapers would disappear, replaced by buildings no more than three or four stories high. Handicapped people could never go above the first floor. Thanks to Elisha Otis people today can continue to go up, and up, and up without climbing stairs.

FACT OR FICTION?

The flashlight grew out of a flowerpot.

There was a young fellow took flight
From Russia one very cold night
He had a great thought
So an idea he bought
And created a handy flashlight.

The flashlight grew out of a flowerpot.

Conrad Hubert (1855?-1928)
His flashlight had 101 uses.

Imagine a poor immigrant from Russia who could not speak English except for a few words. How could he make a living? The year was 1890. Conrad Huber came to the United States to make his fortune, but that fortune seemed out of his reach. He worked at any job that would earn him a meal or two. He sold cigars, he repaired watches, he worked in a restaurant. None of these jobs earned him much money. His pants had empty pockets most of the time.

Hubert had a good friend who was an inventor. His friend, Joshua Cowen, liked to tinker with batteries and wires. One day when Conrad stopped by to visit, Joshua showed him a new invention, a flowerpot that would light up and shine a light on the flower by pushing a button. Surely every housewife would want one. Joshua could produce the pots and Conrad would be the salesman. Unfortunately the new business never got started. Joshua began tinkering with electrical toys. He decided he did not want to make the flowerpots.

Conrad had an idea. If a flowerpot could be lit, why not a hand torch? He bought Joshua's idea for a few dollars and began tinkering on his own. He used paper and a fiber tube, added a bulb and a battery, and in 1898, created "an electric hand torch." It worked but would only flash for a few seconds.

Conrad got a patent on this first flashlight and started the Ever Ready® Battery Company. Conrad's first flashlight was much improved years later when nickel-plated tubes and tungsten filament bulbs were added. The poor immigrant who came to seek his fortune found it. He became a millionaire. In 1916, the company advertised 101 uses for the Ever Ready® flashlight. How many uses can you think of?

FACT OR FICTION?

Benjamin Franklin had only two years of schooling.

There once was a small boy named Ben

Who ceased formal schooling at ten

But continued to look

At book after book

And became the most learn-ed of men!

Benjamin Franklin had only two years of schooling.

Benjamin Franklin (1706-1790)
He could do anything!

"Will that boy ever sit still?" his mother moaned. Ben raced in and out of the house, up and down the stairs, a whirlwind of constant motion. The only time Ben sat still was to learn something new. He was a very curious boy.

In 1716, ten-year-old Ben went to work. *"After all, two years of schooling are enough for any boy,"* his father said. With a wife and 17 children to feed Mr. Franklin needed his 10 boys to earn a wage as soon as they were able. Ben worked for his father, a tallow chandler. Ben found the work dull and boring. The young boy with his bright, inquisitive mind needed a different job.

Ben finally got a job to challenge his mind. He went to work for his brother, James. James was starting a newspaper, and Ben delivered the papers. The curious boy also learned the printing trade. He read everything he could get his hands on. Before long he wrote articles for the paper. One of his articles so upset authorities that his brother, James, was thrown in jail for a month.

Ben was 40 years old before he began to act on the hundreds of ideas in his head. He got tired of looking for his reading glasses so he invented bifocal glasses. That way he could see both near and far without having to take off his glasses. He experimented with electricity and invented the lightning rod. He didn't like cold rooms, so he invented the Franklin Stove. In his spare time he bought and ran his own newspaper, wrote Poor Richard's Almanack, and started the first public library and fire department in Philadelphia. Ben also served his country by traveling to England to talk the English lawmakers into doing away with taxes. He returned home to be one of the committee of five who wrote the Declaration of Independence. As it turned out it was a very good thing that Ben could never sit still!

FACT OR FICTION?

Robert Fulton was a doodler!

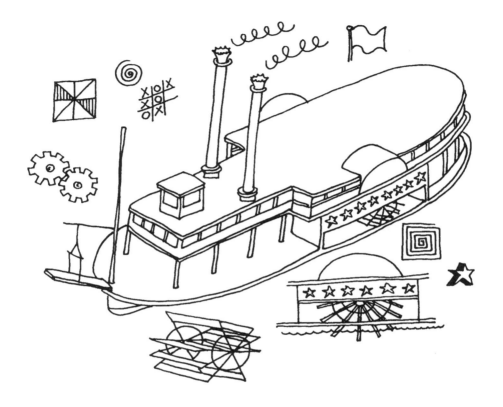

At school Robert's thinking would stray

He daydreamed almost every day

Then he dreamed up a boat

The fastest to float

And the passengers shouted HOORAY!

Robert Fulton was a doodler!

Robert Fulton (1765-1815)
He made river travel faster.

"*Robert, answer the question,*" his teacher demanded. Robert looked up from his daydreaming. He didn't know what the question was. Robert rarely knew what the question was. He daydreamed all the way through school. Sometimes his daydreams took the form of doodles and sketches. Robert did his best thinking when he doodled.

The times he did not daydeam were those times he visited his friend, William Henry. William was a master mechanic who liked inventing things. Machine parts, clocks, and books filled his workshop. Robert spent time putting machine parts together in new ways. William didn't laugh when Robert doodled his ideas.

William was not surprised when Robert grew up to design the first power-driven steamboat. Before his success with the steamboat in 1807, Robert tried several ways to make a living. He painted small portraits and created larger paintings which he sold. He did not make a great deal of money as a painter, so he worked with machines and doodled away until he drew up plans for the first submarine. He actually built the submarine and named it *The Nautilus.* He gave a successful demonstration of his underwater boat in 1800, but no government wanted one.

Robert did not give up. If an underwater boat was not wanted, how about a power-driven "on top of the water" boat? Robert got out his pen and doodled again. As a result, in 1803, he demonstrated a steam-driven boat on the River Seine in France. He then gave the same demonstration on the rivers in New York State. His steamboat traveled an amazing four miles per hour. Five years later Robert built his most successful steamboat, the *Clermont.* It traveled from New York City to Albany in 32 hours. A sailing ship would take three times that long to make the same trip. Thanks to Fulton's doodling, travel in the East was faster and more comfortable than ever before.

One other thing Fulton proved – sometimes it pays to daydream.

FACT OR FICTION?

Robert Goddard's rockets helped win World War II.

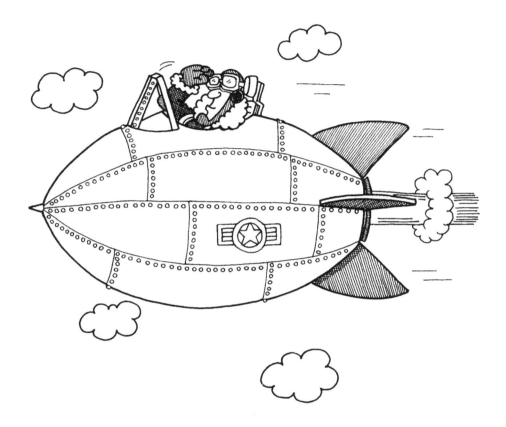

A man built a rocket that flew

A good distance into the blue

His friends gave a laugh

And said he was daft

But what they said just wasn't true.

Robert Goddard's rockets helped win World War II.

Robert Goddard (1882-1945)
The father of modern rocketry

Bang! Pop! Pow! Listen to that noise! Firecrackers went off like machine guns on the Fourth of July, 1902. Robert's friends lit long strings of firecrackers, watching them explode one after another. Robert ignored the noise. When a firecracker exploded, it shot into the air for a short distance. Could a bigger explosion send a rocket into the air? Robert Goddard spent his life trying to find out.

By the age of 25, Goddard was launching rockets from a field on his Aunt Effie's farm. The first rockets fizzled like a match gone out. The neighbors laughed. *"Some crazy fellow is trying to send a rocket to the moon. Imagine that!"* they jeered. Robert paid no attention to the taunts. He went right on building rockets. His persistence paid off. On March 16, 1926, Goddard's 10-foot rocket (named *Nell*) left the ground. It traveled 184 feet landing in a cabbage patch. To Robert's delight it flew 41 feet into the sky!

Still, people made fun of Goddard's rockets. Even the newspapers had unkind things to say. Robert packed up his rockets and headed for New Mexico where he would find vast stretches of land and, best of all, few people. He built rockets that climbed to 9,000 feet. He built rockets that flew faster than sound. By 1939, when war clouds hovered over Europe, Goddard took his rocket ideas to the army. He tried to convince them that rockets could do a lot of damage to an enemy. The army would not listen. Meanwhile, German scientists, who had stolen Goddard's ideas, built rockets that blasted England.

Today the young man that everyone laughed at is called "The Father of Modern Rocketry." He did not live to see the first moon landing, but he knew all the time that it would happen.

FACT OR FICTION?

The Hershey® Bar was developed in a university laboratory.

Young Milton was pinch penny poor

Till his recipe opened a door

He became an All Star

With a great candy bar

When people yelled they wanted more!

The Hershey® Bar was developed in a university laboratory.

Milton S. Hershey (1857- 1945)
He fed the nation's sweet tooth.

The man who invented the Hershey® Bar never saw a university. Milton Hershey came from a poor family and had only a fourth grade education. Milton's father, Henry, was a part-time candymaker and a full-time dreamer. The pennies in the Hershey household were few and far between. At a young age Milton made up his mind to do better than his father. He worked for four years as an apprentice to a local candymaker. He disliked the job, but he learned the skills. When he was 21, Milton went to Philadelphia to make and sell candy. The business failed.

Milton and his father then went to Colorado to strike it rich in the silver mines. Instead of finding a silver mine, Milton found a job with another candymaker. Again, he did not like the job, but he did like the taste of the candy. It was made with fresh milk.

Henry and Milton traveled to Chicago, New Orleans, and New York City. They failed in each city. Milton went home without a penny in his pocket. He borrowed money from an aunt and made caramels with fresh milk. He sold them door to door. People liked the caramels, and Milton earned enough money to start a caramel factory.

Milton was not satisfied to sit on his success. He wanted to do more. He wanted to make milk chocolate that everyone could afford. In 1898, milk chocolate was very expensive. Milton used fresh milk and came up with a recipe that he thought was just right. The people who tried the candy agreed. Best of all, they could buy Milton Hershey's small chocolate bars for five cents. What a bargain!

Milton sold his caramel factory and built a chocolate factory. He also built a town around the factory, with a community center, schools, a hospital, and a beautiful park. The boy with the fourth grade education had become a multi-millionaire!

FACT OR FICTION?

The Hula Hoop saved the jobs of hundreds of workers.

Two chemists found out of the blue

Their test tubes got stuck up with goo

They found that their goop

Made a great hula hoop

Much better than made with bamboo.

The Hula Hoop saved the jobs of hundreds of workers.

Hula Hoop
A craze that took over the world

Have you ever seen pictures of children who lived 100 years ago pushing a big hoop along a sidewalk with a stick? That big hoop was a favorite toy of children long ago. Today children don't push the hoop with a stick. The hoop is twirled round and round the waist. To keep the hoop moving it is necessary to move the body the way a hula dancer dances. That is how it got the name "hula hoop."

Richard (Dick) Knerr and Arthur (Spuds) Melvin had a small company in 1948. They made sling shots in a garage and sold them for less than a dollar. They found that making sling shots was a lot of work with little money coming in. One day they had a visitor from Australia. He told them about bamboo hoops the children played with. Dick and Spuds thought the hoops were a great idea, but they would have to be made of something other than bamboo.

About the same time in 1951, two chemists, Paul Hogan and Robert Banks, were hard at work at the Phillips Petroleum Company. One of their experiments gummed up their testing tubes. They accidentally created a new kind of plastic that would not break when cold or soften with heat. The Phillips Company spent millions of dollars on a new plastics plant. The problem was that no one wanted to buy the new plastic. It was ugly and not always the same size when it came out of the machines. Would the plant close down? Would hundreds of workers lose their jobs?

It was then that Dick and Spuds asked the Phillips Company to make the hula hoops from the new plastic. They planned a sales campaign. Hula hoops were lightweight. The plastic hoops would not break if they were cold or soften if warm. In the next seven years Dick and Spuds sold over a million hula hoops. The new Phillips plant did not close down. Thanks to the hula hoop, hundreds of workers kept their jobs.

FACT OR FICTION?

Horace Wells discovered laughing gas as a pain killer.

One night a young man took his lass

To a show where folks sniffed laughing gas

Then a thought hit his brain

Of a way to kill pain

As a tooth puller he was first class.

Horace Wells discovered laughing gas as a pain killer.

Horace Wells (1815-1848)
The discoverer of anesthesia

It is hard to imagine a time when operations were performed without anything to stop the pain. This was true until in 1844, Horace Wells made an astounding discovery. Horace was a dentist in Hartford, Massachusetts. He did not like causing his patients pain when he found it necessary to pull a tooth. He tried to be as fast as he could extracting the tooth since there were no pain-killers.

Nitrous oxide had been around for a long time. People called it "laughing gas." It was used mainly for entertainment. When members of the audience at a laughing gas show were given a large whiff of nitrous oxide, they would begin laughing and dancing and doing and saying silly things. The audience thought the shows were very funny.

One night in December 1844, Horace took his wife to a laughing gas show. One of the participants got so rowdy that he fell against a bench. When he got up he did not appear to have any pain from the hard fall. That night Horace Wells saw what no one else saw. If the laughing gas could keep the injured man from feeling pain, perhaps it would keep dental patients from feeling pain.

Horace could not wait to try out his discovery. He obtained some laughing gas and asked a dentist friend to pull one of his teeth. The friend did so, and when the laughing gas wore off Horace was thrilled that he had felt no pain.

To make a discovery is one thing. To get others to try it is not easy. Horace demonstrated his discovery at a local hospital. Unfortunately, the patient was not given enough of the gas. Horace pulled the tooth, and the patient yelled. The doctors who watched laughed at Horace's discovery.

Soon after, Horace Wells' student William T. Morton, began using ether to put his patients to sleep before pulling a tooth. He was so successful doctors began using ether in operations. Everyone praised William Morton. Horace Wells never received the credit that was due him for being the first to use anesthesia.

If you should ever visit Hartford, Massachusetts, and take a stroll through Bushnell Park, stop for a moment at the statue of Horace Wells, and thank him for the pain-free surgery and dentistry we have today!

FACT OR FICTION?

Marconi, inventor of the telegraph, failed his university entrance exams.

There once was a boy who took care

In sending a message by air

He made signals dance

From England to France

An invention he wanted to share.

Fact 17

Marconi, inventor of the telegraph, failed his university entrance exams.

Guglielmo Marconi (1874-1937)
He made wireless signals travel the world.

"That boy is a good for nothing! If he thinks I will support him all his life while he plays in the attic he is sadly mistaken." These words might have been spoken by Guglielmo Marconi's wealthy father who thought his son to be a foolish dreamer.

The attic where Guglielmo "played" was actually a laboratory the boy had built to carry out experiments with wireless signals. As a bookworm he read about the possibility of sending signals through the air without wires. The idea had such appeal he was determined to see if he could make it work. As a teenager he attended school at the Leghorn Technical Institute where he devoted nearly all of his time to the study of physics. Unfortunately, he did not know enough about other subjects to pass the entrance exam to the University of Bologna. He had to continue learning on his own.

Guglielmo had a willing brother to help him with his experiments. After countless experiments and many failures, he developed both a transmitter and a receiver that sent wireless signals short distances. Guglielmo would ask his brother to take a receiver greater and greater distances away while he sent signals. If the brother was out of sight he would shoot a shotgun to show he received the signal. Within a short time Guglielmo sent wireless signals over a distance of more than 10 miles. By age 25 he perfected his wireless system to send signals from England to France. Two years later he sent signals across the Atlantic, a distance of more than 2,000 miles.

In 1909, the "good-for-nothing" boy who failed the University entrance exams was awarded the Nobel Prize for Physics. Marconi had made the world smaller by making communication among people and nations fast and easy.

FACT OR FICTION?

The first friction match was three feet long.

Some chemicals stirred in a pot

On a stick proceeded to clot

The mixture would hatch

The first friction match

Whether expected or not.

The first friction match was three feet long.

John Walker
His match was an accident.

Suppose you spent years trying to invent one thing but discovered something entirely different. That is what happened to John Walker. In 1826, John was a chemist who lived and worked in England. Day after day he worked in his laboratory to come up with a safer and more effective explosive. He experimented with many different chemicals, but none gave him the result he wanted. One day John was mixing two chemicals, stirring them with a stick. Part of the gooey mixture hardened on the end of the stick. John took the stick and rubbed it against the floor to get the hardened glob off. To his surprise the stick burst into flame. John's three-foot-long stick was the first friction match. This was probably a very good thing, since these first matches were very dangerous to use.

It wasn't until 30 years later that matches became safe to use. Johan Lundstrom of Sweden discovered a way to strike the match against phosphorus coating on a matchbox. He called his invention a "safety match."

Seventy five years after John Walker made his amazing discovery, a Philadelphia lawyer who smoked cigars came up with the idea of book matches. Joshua Pusey had little room in his pockets for the large box of matches he needed to light his cigars. If the matches were made of paper instead of wood they would be small enough to carry around. Joshua worked and worked on his idea and invented the first book matches. They were small. They were easy to use, and they took up little room in a pocket.

One would think that everyone would have welcomed Joshua's new book matches. They did not. He tried for more than five years to sell his idea, but no one wanted his book matches. Then an opera company wanted to advertise and put their name on Joshua's small match books. The matches became a success.

FACT OR FICTION?

"The Real McCoy" was an invention by a cowboy hero.

There once was a most clever boy

Who discovered a way to his joy

To give each moving coil

A good squirt of oil

And they called it "The Real McCoy."

The "Real McCoy" was an invention by a cowboy hero.

Elijah McCoy (1843-1929)
His lubricating system was "The Real McCoy."

To be a fugitive is to escape from something. Elijah McCoy's parents were fugitive slaves. George and Mildred McCoy escaped from slavery and made their way to Canada where they could live as free people. Their son, Elijah, was born in Canada in 1843. Elijah's parents worked hard to give Elijah the education that neither of them had. The family moved to Michigan when Elijah was a boy. George McCoy worked as a logger and saved enough money to send fifteen-year-old Elijah to school in Scotland.

Elijah worked hard at his studies and returned to the United States as a fully qualified engineer. Sad to say he could not find work. No one would hire a black mechanical engineer. Elijah took a job as an oilman and fireman for the Michigan Central Railroad. Train travel was slow in those days, because the train would have to stop often while the oilman got out and oiled the moving parts. Elijah thought there must be a way to oil the moving parts while the train was in motion. By 1872, he had invented a cup and tube that would allow any machine to be oiled without stopping. Elijah's invention was such a success that anyone buying a new machine would ask first if it contained "The Real McCoy."

Elijah went on to invent many other things. Housewives can thank him for the first ironing board. Many gardeners do not know that Elijah McCoy invented the first lawn sprinkler system.

Elijah made very little money from his inventions. As he got older he lost the little money he had and became ill. He died in a charity hospital in 1929, a forgotten man. Only recently has Elijah McCoy been recognized as the man who changed forever the machine industry by allowing the machines to be oiled without stopping.

FACT OR FICTION?

The microwave oven was an accident.

A new way to cook Percy gave

That caused all the people to rave

In his pocket he felt

A candy bar melt

The start of the first microwave.

The microwave oven was an accident.

Percy L. Spencer (1894-1970)
A chocolate bar melted in his pocket.

In 1940, the people who lived in London, England, cringed at a familiar sound. The shrill whistles of air raid warnings filled the air. Everyone rushed to underground shelters waiting to hear the explosions as enemy planes dropped their bombs. Then came the discovery of radar. Radar beams could find the position of a plane as well as its speed and direction. Radar stations with their huge magnetron tubes were set up all along the English coast. Planes could be detected and stopped before reaching London.

One of the makers of the magnetron tubes was the Raytheon Company in the United States. One of its scientists was Percy L. Spencer. He invented a remote control tube for his young son's model plane. The same tube sent shells to enemy targets in World War II.

One day Percy was working in his laboratory at Raytheon. Nearby were several large magnetron tubes. Percy was hungry. He remembered that he had a candy bar in his pocket. To his surprise, his fingers dug in his pocket to find a gooey mess. The candy bar had melted. Percy asked for other foods to be brought into the laboratory. The other workers thought he had a big appetite. Instead of eating the foods he held them near the magnetron tubes. Popcorn began to pop. The microwaves from the tubes produced heat that cooked the food. Not only did the waves cook the food, they cooked it faster than ever before.

Percy showed the bosses at Raytheon his discovery. The bosses knew a good thing when they saw it. In 1947, Raytheon perfected the first microwave oven. It weighed 750 pounds and was as big as a refrigerator. It would be 20 years before a small enough oven was made to fit into homes.

The next time you pop popcorn in the microwave, thank Percy Spencer for being curious enough to find out why his candy bar melted.

FACT OR FICTION?

Anton Leeuwenhoek shared his invention of the microscope with others.

With glass lenses Anton would try

To answer the question of why

When his sharp gaze would pass

Through a thick lens of glass

He saw worlds not seen with the eye.

Anton Leeuwenhoek shared his invention of the microscope with others.

Anton Leeuwenhoek (1632-1723)
He saw things no one else could see.

"Don't bother going to Anton's store," the ladies of Delft said. *"He probably won't be there."* They were usually right.

Anton Leeuwenhoek was a Dutch storekeeper who did not like keeping a store. The people of Delft never knew whether the store would be open or not. The store sold clothing, pins, needles, and cloth among other things. Anton was not interested in pins, or needles, or cloth. He was interested in small convex lenses that he made of different thicknesses. He slid the lenses between brass plates to see things that had never before been seen.

The people of Delft thought Anton was addle-brained. They were sure he had no sense at all, playing all day with his glass lenses. He should have been working hard in the store earning a living for his family. After all, he was not a scientist. He was not a doctor. He had no scientific education.

Anton did not listen to his critics. He went on making the lenses and peering though them. He studied the brains and the life cycles of insects. He discovered that weevils and fleas did not grow from wheat seeds but from tiny eggs. He discovered that a single drop of water contained more than one type of living bacteria. Through his glass lenses Anton could magnify objects up to 300 times and was able to give the first accurate description of red blood cells.

Anton Leeuwenhoek was considered crazy by those who knew him, but he is known today as the inventor of the microscope. Did he share his invention with others? He did not. Anton kept secret the methods he used to make his lenses. It would be another hundred years before the first really useful microscopes were created.

FACT OR FICTION?

Samuel Morse was awarded a gold medal for his art.

As a painter he ran out of cash

So invented the dot and the dash

In a one-wire mode

He sent Morse Code

And the message arrived in a flash.

Samuel Morse was awarded a gold medal for his art.

Samuel F. B. Morse (1791-1872)
He invented the one-wire telegraph and Morse Code.

No one predicted that Samuel Morse would be remembered for the series of dots and dashes he used to send messages. People who knew Samuel said he would be remembered as a famous painter.

Samuel showed his talent for art at an early age. If lessons in school were boring, Samuel could be found sketching whatever caught his eye. His later studies were not in electricity but in art as he attended the Royal Academy of Art in London. While there he won a gold medal for his statue of the Dying Hercules.

Morse knew that the rest of his life would be devoted to painting. However, winning the gold medal did not send people flocking to his door. For four years he tried to earn a living with his art in England but could not support himself. He returned to New York where he was more successful and became a well-known portrait painter.

When Samuel was in his early forties he began experimenting with the telegraph. It was a subject that had always interested him. He knew that pulses of electric current could travel over wires. At that time a telegraph needed twenty-six wires to send a message. Samuel worked on a one-wire telegraph for 10 years. At the same time, with the help of his assistant, Alfred Vail, he devised a code of dots and dashes to represent letters of the alphabet and required only one wire to send. Some say that Alfred Vail did most of the work on the code.

Samuel Morse did not invent the telegraph, but he did improve on it. He also convinced the United States Congress to vote money for "wiring" the United States. The amount was small, but Samuel gave numerous demonstrations of his telegraph and convinced many private companies to build telegraph lines.

It was not long before the lines covered more than 20,000 miles. Samuel Morse had shown that his one-line telegraph and Morse Code did work. Because of the work of Samuel Morse the United States became a little smaller as communication became much faster.

FACT OR FICTION?

Alfred Nobel, the inventor of dynamite, gave money for a peace prize.

Nobel got his figures just right

He invented a safe dynamite

It caused quite a shock

Making mountains of rock

A truly spectacular sight.

Alfred Nobel, the inventor of dynamite, gave money for a peace prize.

Alfred Nobel (1833-1896)
He made a big bang!

Each year a great honor, the Nobel Peace prize, is given to the person who has done the most to bring about world peace. The money for the prize comes from the nine million dollars left in his will by Alfred Nobel. To some it may seem strange that the inventor of dynamite cared greatly about world peace. Alfred Nobel, who loved writing poetry, always intended that his invention, dynamite, be used for peaceful purposes, not for war.

Alfred Nobel was born in Sweden but moved with his family to Russia when he was 11 years old. His father had a lot of money, and Alfred and his brothers did not attend public schools. They were taught at home. Alfred liked the lessons in languages and literature. The young dreamer spent most of his time writing poems.

Alfred's father was not happy with his poet son. As a teenager, Alfred could speak and write German, Swedish, English, French, and Russian. His father still was not pleased. Speaking other languages and writing poems would not get Alfred a good job. He sent Alfred to school in Paris. There Alfred was to work hard at his studies and be trained as a chemical engineer.

In Paris, Alfred learned about nitroglycerine, a powerful and dangerous explosive that could blast through mountains. Alfred returned to Sweden to experiment with nitroglycerine. One of his experiments caused a building to blow up. The government declared that no more experiments were to be done in the city. Alfred moved out to a barge on the lake. There he found a way to mix the dangerous explosive with a fine sand. He shaped the sandy paste into rods which could be placed in drilled holes to blast away rock. He called the rods dynamite.

Alfred's invention meant that tunnels and roads could be safely built through mountains of hard rock. He also invented a safe way to set off the explosions. Construction workers would be safer than ever before. The boy who wanted to be remembered as a great poet never dreamed he would be remembered as the inventor of dynamite.

FACT OR FICTION?

André Garnerin used a parachute
to escape from prison.

There once was a man who took flight

In a parachute from a great height

It spun round and round

Till it reached the ground

And gave the crowds watching a fright.

André Garnerin used a parachute to escape from prison.

André Jacques Garnerin (1769-1823)
He made more than 200 parachute jumps.

How does a man spend his time in prison? In 1792, André Garnerin paced back and forth in a prison cell in Hungary. The prison had walls so high that a man could be killed trying to jump from them. André studied the problem of escaping over the walls. If something could be constructed to slow the fall from the walls, then a man might not be injured. André drew up plans for cloth stretched over a frame large enough to hold up a man. Before he could use his plan to escape André was released from prison. Now he could see if his parachute idea worked.

André's first parachute resembled a huge umbrella with cloth stretched over ribs. The year was 1797. He hired a balloon with a basket to take him to a height of 3,000 feet. When the balloon rose high enough, André cut the cords to the balloon. Down, down the basket went twirling round and round. André landed safely but with a terrible case of motion sickness.

André tried his invention again and again. Each time the balloon rose higher than before. Crowds gasped when he remained in the basket after having cut the ropes to the balloon. They watched in awe as the basket spun round and round and slowly descended to earth. André's wife thought this looked like fun. She wanted to try André's invention. In 1799, she made the first parachute jump by a woman.

André wanted to show his invention to everyone. He traveled throughout Europe thrilling crowds with more than 200 daring jumps. He did get attention but not the kind he wanted. The newspapers of the day made fun of André. Surely there could be no practical use for such a silly stunt. To put one's life in danger for no reason seemed the height of foolishness.

In 1799, neither the newspapers nor André could guess that the invention of the airplane nearly 100 years later would make his invention of the parachute the life saver that it came to be.

FACT OR FICTION?

An angry cook invented potato chips.

A diner let cook know his wish

He wanted thin fries with his fish

Cook with a mean grin

Made chips paper thin

And created a popular dish.

An angry cook invented potato chips.

George Crum
His temper got the best of him.

George Crum had a temper. He was a Native American who worked as a guide, a trapper, and a cook in upper New York State. Most people who knew him described George Crum as a tough character.

In 1853, George was working as a cook at the fancy Moon Lake Lodge in Saratoga Springs, New York. One thing that got George's temper up was a customer who sent food back to the kitchen with a complaint. By the time angry George "fixed up" the returned meal and sent it back to the diner, it looked or smelled so bad that it could not be eaten. It was never a good idea to complain to George about his cooking.

Legend says that Cornelius Vanderbilt, one of the wealthiest men in the nation, dined one night at the Moon Lake Lodge. He did not know about George Crum's temper when he ordered fried potatoes. The potatoes were not to Vanderbilt's liking. He sent them back to the kitchen saying that they were too thick. At first the cook held his temper. He knew Vanderbilt was an important guest at the Lodge. He sliced potatoes thinner and sent them back. Once again the plate was returned to the kitchen. The potatoes were still too thick!

George Crum lost his temper. He sliced potatoes in paper thin slices. He fried them so crispy that they could not be picked up with a fork. He grabbed the salt shaker and gave them a good dose of salt. Back the potatoes went to Cornelius Vanderbilt. George waited for the explosion. He knew he would probably lose his job. But no explosion came. The potato chips were delicious! Everyone at Vanderbilt's table wanted to try them.

The Moon Lake Lodge added potato chips to its menu. Not long after, George Crum opened his own restaurant. Can you guess what the featured item on the menu was? You guessed correctly. Potato Chips!

FACT OR FICTION?

The invention of the printing press
made Gutenberg
a wealthy man.

The printing press sat on a stand

And printed out books on demand

Then folks saw the need

To learn how to read

When books were not copied by hand.

Fiction 17

The invention of the printing press made Gutenberg a wealthy man.

Johannes Gutenberg (1400?-1468)
His printing press changed the world.

If you wanted to go to the library in the 1400s you were out of luck. There were no libraries, because there were so few books. At that time books were copied by hand or stamped from text cut into wood, usually by monks. The books, because they were so rare, were kept under lock and key in monasteries. Not too many people of that time were bothered that there were so few books, because so few people knew how to read.

Johannes Gutenberg changed all that. He was a goldsmith in Strasburg, Germany, who taught his pupils how to make eyeglasses and polish gems. He also was a printer who knew that copying books by hand or cutting words into a wooden block were not the best ways to produce a book. There had to be a better way.

Johannes decided that making letters out of metal would be a practical way to print. The metal letters would be moved around to spell different words. These letters would last a long time. Because they could be moved from one place to another, they could be used again and again.

Johannes had very little money. He wanted to design and build a printing press with hundreds of metal letters. Johannes had a friend, Johann Fust, who loaned him the money he needed. After two years of hard work Johannes produced his first printed book, the Gutenberg Bible.

As soon as the Bible was finished, Fust wanted his money back. When he did not get it, he took possession of the printing press and movable type. Johannes made no money from his invention.

The printing press did change people's lives. When printed books became available, worlds of knowledge opened up to all who could read. It was the beginning of a new age, the Age of Print!

FACT OR FICTION?

The refrigerator was invented for yellow fever patients.

John Gorrie followed one rule

His patients got better when cool

His machine that made ice

Was really quite nice

Though newspapers called him a fool.

The refrigerator was invented for yellow fever patients.

Dr. John Gorrie (1802-1855)
He wanted to cool off his patients.

It is hard to imagine a time when there were no refrigerators. Fresh meat had to be eaten at once or not at all. Milk would spoil within a day. There were no refrigerators in 1833, when Dr. John Gorrie arrived in Apalachicola, Florida. It was a hot, muggy town. Nearby were swamps where mosquitoes bred. Many people got sick. No one knew that the bite of some mosquitoes caused yellow fever. Dr. Gorrie knew that he saw fewer patients with yellow fever in cooler months and more in the warmer months.

Dr. Gorrie figured that keeping a room cool might help his yellow fever patients. He rigged up a tub of ice and hung it from the ceiling of the sick room. Ice was not easy to find in Florida. It was brought packed in sawdust by boat from frozen lakes in the North. It melted quickly in the hot Florida climate.

"What if there was a way to make ice?" Dr. Gorrie wondered. He knew that when liquid evaporates, it cools the air around it. Working night and day Dr. Gorrie built a compressor that would do the same with gas. As the gas slowly evaporated, it would cool the surrounding air. By controlling the rate of evaporation ice formed.

Dr. Gorrie found a friend to put up the needed money to build his ice machine. In Cincinnati, he found a company willing to produce the machine. Things looked just fine until the newspapers heard about it. Instead of welcoming an ice machine they made fun of it. The friend who invested money died. The company that agreed to make the machine changed its mind.

Dr. Gorrie went back to Florida thinking himself a failure. Little did he know that his ice machine would lead the way to modern refrigerators and air conditioned homes and offices.

FACT OR FICTION?

The first traffic light had three lights - stop, go, and caution.

A fellow named Morgan was right

Crossing streets was a terrible fright

He had safety to gain

When he used his quick brain

Inventing the first traffic light.

The first traffic signal had three lights - stop, go, and caution.

Garrett Morgan (1875-1963)
The man who saved many lives

On July 25, 1916, a terrible explosion took place in an underground tunnel. Thirty-two men were trapped in the tunnel which was difficult to reach. It was 250 feet beneath Lake Erie. Garrett Morgan, the son of former slaves, led the rescue party using the new gas masks he had invented. The men were saved. The gas masks were so successful that both fire departments and the army wanted them.

Garrett was a bright boy who grew up on the family farm in Kentucky. He attended elementary school but as a teenager went to Ohio to find work. He continued to learn with private lessons that he paid for. Garrett was handy with machines. He worked as a repairman for a sewing machine company. By the time he was 32 years old he owned his own repair shop. He was so successful he opened a tailor shop and bought a newspaper. He bought an automobile and taught himself to drive. Garrett Morgan was fast becoming a well-to-do man.

By 1920, automobiles had been around only a few years. Most people traveled by horse and buggy or horse-drawn wagons. Imagine what would happen if an automobile and a horse-drawn wagon turned a corner at the same time! There were many accidents. People were afraid to cross a street. An automobile traveling at a great speed of 20 miles an hour might knock them down. Garrett saw a car hit a wagon right in front of him. Then and there he decided that something had to be done to make the streets safer. He invented the traffic signal. There were no caution or left turn lights. It had a light for stop, a light for go, and a light that allowed people to walk safely across the street. Every modern city in the nation wanted Garrett Morgan's traffic light.

Thanks to Garrett Morgan, many lives have been saved because of his invention. The boy with a grade school education made not just the United States safer, but the world, as his traffic light was installed in nearly every country where there were automobiles.

FACT OR FICTION?

Velcro® came about from
a walk in the woods.

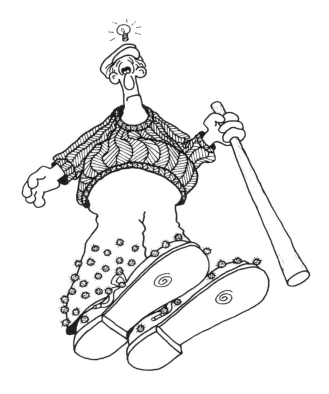

A young man took a walk in the rain

Found cockleburs could be a pain

Till he took a good look

At the tiny burr's hook

And a Velcro® idea hit his brain.

Velcro® came about from a walk in the woods.

George de Mestral
He invented Velcro®.

A long walk through the woods means pants and shirts are covered with co
ckleburs which must be picked off one at a time. What is it that makes them cling so tightly to clothing? It is amazing that through the centuries when people and cockleburs have met that no one asked that question until 1948.

In 1948, a scientist was walking through the Swiss woods. His name was George de Mestral. Like most scientists he had a natural curiosity. When his walk was finished he, like everyone else, picked the cockleburs off his clothing. But then he asked the important question. What made the burrs stick? George placed a cocklebur under his microscope. What he saw amazed him. Each cocklebur was made up of many tiny hooks. It was the hooks that grabbed onto the walker's clothing.

George had a great idea! Here was a new way to fasten clothing rather than the traditional buttons or zippers. It took him many years of trial and error before he came up with his invention which he called Velcro®. The invention required a strip of fabric with tiny hooks and a strip of soft or plush fabric. The Velcro® could be used to fasten almost any kind of clothing. It was strong. It was easy to use, and it could be washed. It was patented in 1955.

He set up the first Velcro® factory in Switzerland. The new fastener was so popular that an American factory was opened five years later. George's walk in the woods, combined with his natural curiosity, had made him a wealthy man.

The next time you walk in the woods, keep your eyes open. Like George de Mestral, you never know what you might discover.

FACT OR FICTION?

Neither of the Wright Brothers received a high school diploma.

Two brothers whose last names were Wright

Desired to make a manned flight

With hard work and care

Put a plane in the air

To prove to the world they were right!

Neither of the Wright Brothers received a high school diploma.

Wilbur Wright (1867- 1912) Orville Wright (1871-1948)
They made the world smaller.

It is true that neither Wilbur nor Orville Wright received a high school diploma, but both were life long learners. The brothers were two of the six children of Bishop Milton Wright and his wife, Susan. In the Wright household curiosity was encouraged. If the boys had a question they could go to the well-stocked library. Wilbur did not receive his high school diploma, because the family moved. Orville gave up the traditional high school studies after three years to study on his own.

Wilbur and Orville played with the idea of flight from childhood. When Wilbur was 11 and Orville seven they were given a flying toy by a friend of their father's. If the small machine could fly, why couldn't a full-sized machine manned by a person fly?

At age 19, Wilbur was accidentally hit with a baseball bat. For four years he was a semi-invalid. Dreams of college were given up, but his dream of one day building a flying machine stayed close to his heart.

In 1892, the brothers opened the Wright Cycle Company in Dayton, Ohio. To earn a living they sold and repaired bicycles. It was a good business, and any profit from the shop went into the project in the back room. They were building an airplane. Orville was as enthusiastic about the idea as Wilbur.

As each difficulty arose they found a way to solve the problem. They designed and re-designed the shape of the wings. They built their own wind tunnel. They designed props and built their own gas-powered, lightweight engine.

After four years of hard work they were ready for the first flight. Orville was to make the flight and control the plane. On December 17, 1903, the plane took off from Kitty Hawk, North Carolina. The flight lasted 12 seconds and traveled a distance of 120 feet. The age of aviation had begun. The world had become smaller in just 12 seconds!

ADDITIONAL READING

Better mousetraps : product improvements that led to success by Nathan Aaseng. Lerner Publications. Group, 1990.

Black inventors by Nathan Aaseng. Facts-On-File, 1997.

Biography today: Scientists & inventors series, Vol. 5: profiles of people of interest to young readers by Cherie D. Abbey. Omnigraphics, Inc., 2001.

Biography today: Scientists & inventors series, Vol. 8 : profiles of people of interest to young readers by Cherie D. Abbey. Omnigraphics, Inc., 2002. 2003.

Communications: sending the message by Thomas Streissguth. Oliver Press, 1997.

Dreamers & doers: inventors who changed our world by Norman Richards. Atheneum, 1984.

Eureka! it's a telephone! by Jeannne Bendick. Millbrook Press, 1993.

Eureka! it's an airplane! by Jeannne Bendick. Millbrook Press, 1992.

Eureka! it's an automobile! by Jeannne Bendick. Millbrook Press, 1992.

Everyday inventions by Meredith Hooper. Taplinger Pub. Co., 1976.

Everyday things by Chris Oxlade. Franklin Watts, 1994.

The evolution of useful things (1st Edition) by Henry Petroski. Knopf, 1992.

Great discoveries and inventions by David Lambert and Jane Insley. Facts-On-File, 1985.

Great discoveries & inventions that advanced industry and technology by Antonio Casanellas. Gareth Stevens, 2000.

Great discoveries and inventions that improved our daily lives by Antonio Casanellas. Gareth Stevens, 2000.

Industrial Revolution: Biographies by James Outman. UXL Publishers, 2003.

Invention by Lionel Bender. Knopf, 1991.

Invention & discovery by Struan Reid. Usborne, 1987.

Invention and technology by Pope John Paul II and Milton Lomask. Simon & Schuster children's Publishing, 1992.

Inventive genius by the editors of Time-Life Books, 1991.

Inventors who left their brands on America by Frank Olsen. Bantam, 1991.

Mistakes that worked (1st Edition) by Charlotte Jones. Doubleday, 1991.

Nineteenth Century Inventors by Jon Noonan. Facts On File, 1992.

Really useful : the origins of everyday things by Joel Levy. Firefly Books, 2002.

Small inventions that make a big difference David J. Crup, Editor. National Geographic Society, 1984.

Steven Caney's invention book. by Steven Caney. Workman, 1985.

The story of things by Frank Jupo. Prentice Hall, 1972.

The story of things by Kate Morgan. Walker & Company, 1991.

Toilets, toasters & telephones: the how and why of everyday objects by Susan Goldman Rubin. Harcourt, 1998.

What does it do?: inventions then and now by Daniel Jacobs. Heinemann Library, 1990.

Why didn't I think of that?: From alarm clocks to zippers by Webb Garrison. Prentice-Hall, 1977.